RO'   'S

F   ɔ

A young artist's guide

PFT

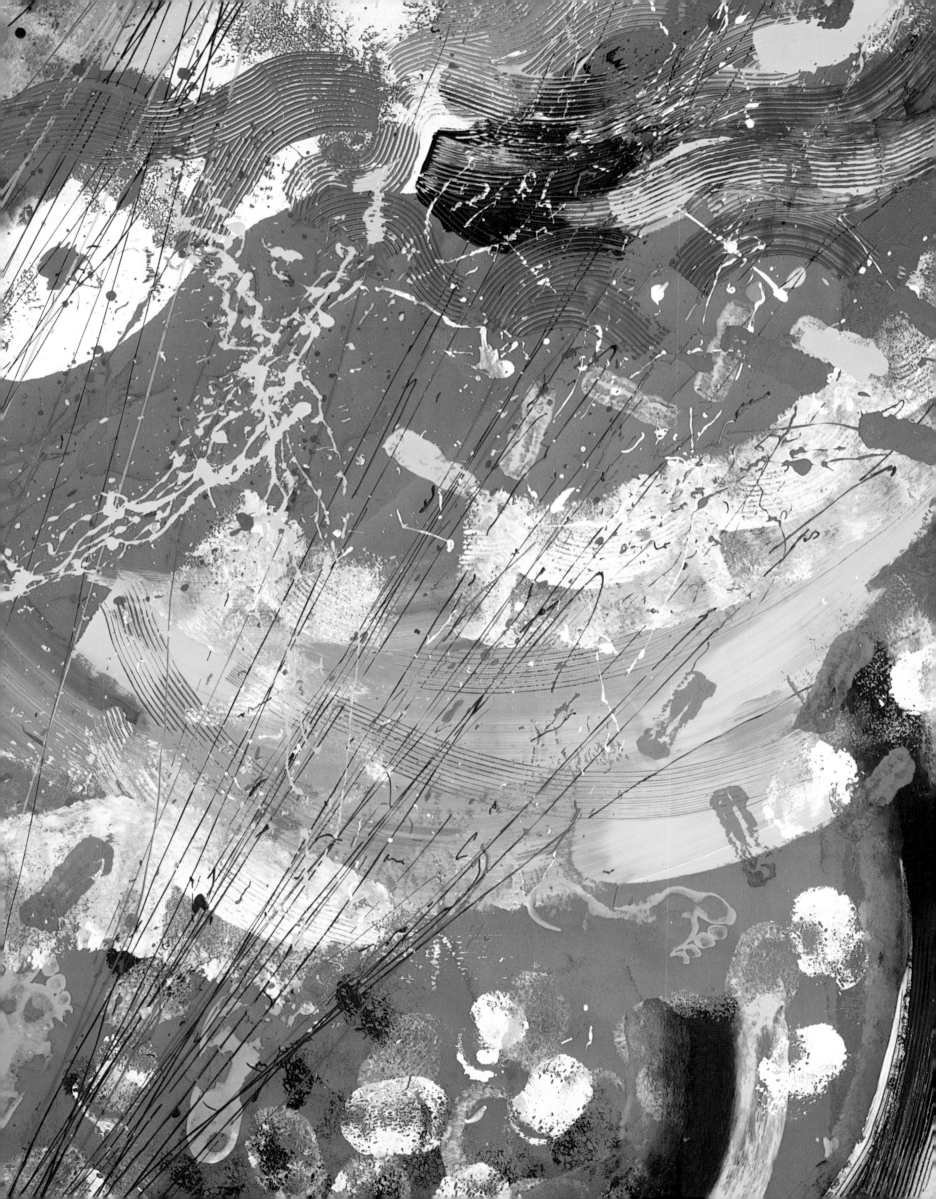

ROYAL ACADEMY OF ARTS
Painting
A young artist's guide

Elizabeth Waters & Annie Harris

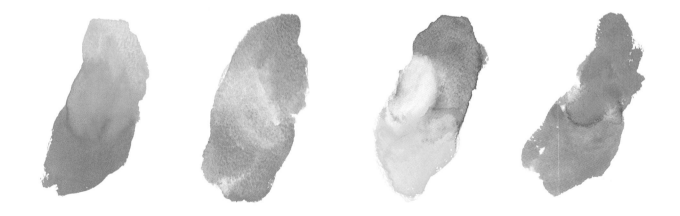

DK

DORLING KINDERSLEY
London • New York • Moscow • Sydney

A DORLING KINDERSLEY BOOK

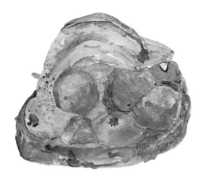

For Charles and Edna Waters
For Greg, Zoe, and Tabby Harris

Editor Helen Drew
Art Editor Karen Fielding

Managing Editor Jane Yorke
Managing Art Editor Chris Scollen
Picture Research Lorna Ainger
Production Shelagh Gibson

Photography Dave King
Diagrams Coral Mula

First published in Great Britain
by Dorling Kindersley Limited, London
9 Henrietta Street, London WC2E 8PS

First paperback edition

2 4 6 8 10 9 7 5 3 1

A CIP catalogue record for this book is available from
the British Library.

ISBN 0-7513-5741-3

Colour reproduction by Colourscan, Singapore
Printed and bound in Sinapore by Imago

WARNING:
Do not put painting
materials or tools
near your mouth as
some are poisonous.

Contents

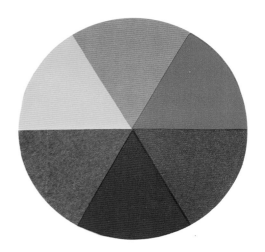

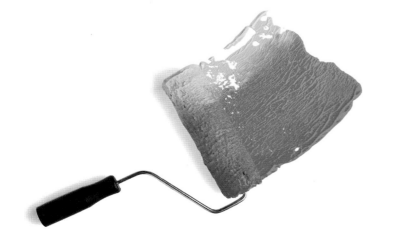

Introduction to painting

People have painted since prehistoric times because painting is a way of showing others how you see the world and what you feel about it. Paint is an expressive, exciting, and colourful substance. There are other ways of making art, such as drawing and sculpting, but this book helps you to explore what is special about painting. Each page introduces an aspect of painting such as shape, movement, or composition, and encourages you to look out for these things in your world and in other artists' work.

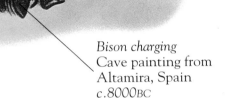

Early painters
The earliest paintings were of wild animals such as this bison. The paintings were rubbed on to cave walls, with colours made from soils and burnt wood, by hunters. They hoped that the images would magically help them in their hunt for food.

Bison charging
Cave painting from Altamira, Spain
*c.8000*BC

Going to galleries
We can only show photographs of paintings on these pages, so you may like to go and find original paintings by some of the artists in a gallery or museum. When you see the paintings, you may be surprised to discover how different their actual size, colour, and texture makes them seem.

PIERO DELLA FRANCESCA
The Nativity c.1472

Learning from other artists
In this book, you will find paintings by artists from different times and countries. Try making a sketch of a painting in order to understand it better, or use one to inspire a painting of your own. Below you can see a painting by five children (aged 9), based on Piero's *The Nativity*.

Looking at paintings
When paintings are hanging in galleries, you may see links between one painting and another. The closer you look at a painting, the more you will notice.

STUART, DENZAL, MICHELLE, JESSICA, GRAHAM, DANIEL *The Nativity 1993*

Painting ideas

On each page you will find paintings, diagrams, practical activities, and subjects for paintings. Whether you prefer to make a painting that is like a window on to a "real" scene, or create an abstract painting with just brushmarks and colours, this book contains a wide range of painting ideas to try.

Collecting resources

On some pages you will find examples of resources. Make your own collection to inspire your paintings.

Paints and brushes
Experiment with the different paints and brushes you can see in this book.

Step by step

Step-by-step photographs and instructions show you painting ideas in action and give practical advice. Use these activities as starting-points for your own painting experiments.

The paintbrush symbol

Where you see this sign, you will find a painting idea to try, or a suggestion for a subject to paint. If you remember to use ideas shown on previous pages, you will soon build up confidence in your painting.

Fresh ideas
All sorts of things can give you fresh ideas about colour, shape, pattern, and texture, and they can feed your imagination.

Painting on your own

Remember that whether a painting is done in oils or poster paint, on a wall or on a piece of paper, it is really just a simple, flat surface that you can fill in any way you like. There is no right or wrong way to paint. Even if you and your friend both paint the same subject, your pictures will be very different because you each see things in your own way.

HELEN (aged 9)
My Bedroom 1993
Compare these paintings by two young artists of their bedrooms.

ELIZABETH (aged 9) *Parrot 1993*
Look for colourful subjects to paint.

LILLY (aged 9) *My Bedroom 1993*
How would you paint your bedroom?

The painter's palette

Most of the paints used by artists today have been in use for thousands of years. Paint is made from pigments (powdered colours), which come from rocks, earth, plants, fruit, insects, and shellfish, or from chemicals. The pigment is ground into a fine powder and is then mixed with a liquid, such as oil or water. This process used to be carried out by an artist's apprentice in the studio, but in the 19th century, tubes of ready-made paints became available. Below, you can see examples of the different types of paint and a selection of the many colours you can buy.

Thumbs up
A palette is held by putting your thumb up through the hole in the middle.

Monet's palette
This is the palette of Claude Monet, the 19th-century Impressionist painter. He used the new bright colours which you can see arranged on this palette.

How oil paint is made

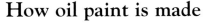

1 First, a substance such as cinnabar is needed. This was used to make vermilion pigment.

2 The pigment is ground into a fine powder by a machine, or by hand with a pestle and mortar.

3 The ground pigment is worked into oil to form a paste on a sheet of glass, using a tool called a muller.

4 Finally, when the paint is thoroughly mixed, it is put into a tube or on to a palette. It is then ready to use.

GIOVANNI BOCCACCIO *Artist with Male Apprentice*
This picture from a 15th-century manuscript shows a woman painting while her apprentice makes paints with a muller. Notice the animal-skin palette and paint stored in shells.

Types of paint

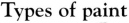

Watercolours
These paints come in tubes or hard blocks. The pigments are ground very fine and mixed with gum. The colours are transparent when mixed with water.

Gouache
Gouache is opaque watercolour. The pigment is thickened with white chalk.

Poster paints
These are cheaply-produced pots of thick, gouache-like paint, used with water.

Inks
Inks are transparent dyes. They come in beautiful colours, but they fade with time.

Acrylics
These can be used thick or thin with water. They dry very quickly.

Oils
These are used with white spirit or turps. You can buy opaque and transparent oils.

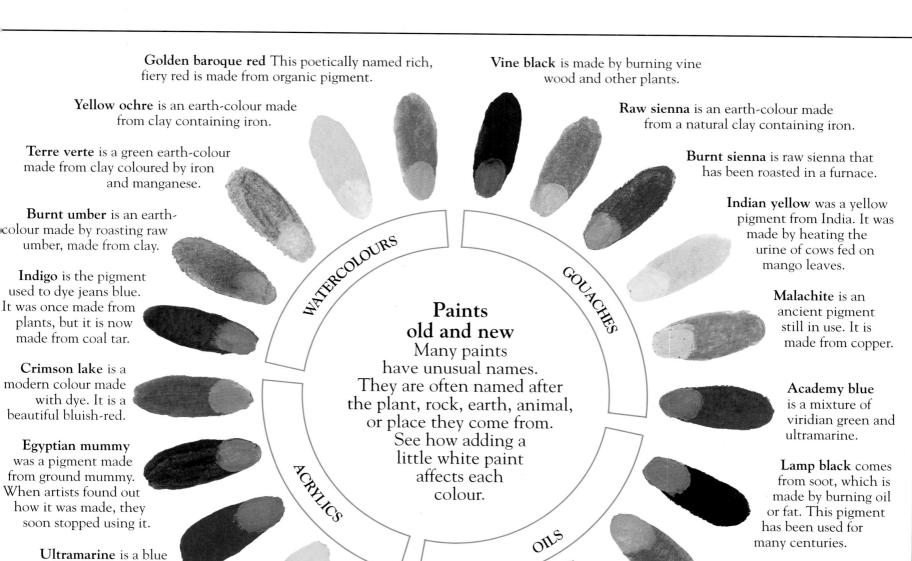

Golden baroque red This poetically named rich, fiery red is made from organic pigment.

Yellow ochre is an earth-colour made from clay containing iron.

Terre verte is a green earth-colour made from clay coloured by iron and manganese.

Burnt umber is an earth-colour made by roasting raw umber, made from clay.

Indigo is the pigment used to dye jeans blue. It was once made from plants, but it is now made from coal tar.

Crimson lake is a modern colour made with dye. It is a beautiful bluish-red.

Egyptian mummy was a pigment made from ground mummy. When artists found out how it was made, they soon stopped using it.

Ultramarine is a blue paint which used to be made from lapis lazuli, a semi-precious stone. It is now made from a chemical.

Naples yellow is made with lead and is poisonous.

Vermilion was made from ground cinnabar, but is now prepared from chemicals.

Tyrian purple was made from crushed shellfish. This expensive pigment was used to dye the robes of the emperors of Ancient Rome.

Vine black is made by burning vine wood and other plants.

Raw sienna is an earth-colour made from a natural clay containing iron.

Burnt sienna is raw sienna that has been roasted in a furnace.

Indian yellow was a yellow pigment from India. It was made by heating the urine of cows fed on mango leaves.

Malachite is an ancient pigment still in use. It is made from copper.

Academy blue is a mixture of viridian green and ultramarine.

Lamp black comes from soot, which is made by burning oil or fat. This pigment has been used for many centuries.

Cerulean blue is a bright sky-blue, made from a mineral.

Rose madder is a ruby-red pigment made from the madder plant.

Dragon's blood was the name of a pigment made from a fruit. People thought that it was made from real dragon's blood.

WATERCOLOURS

GOUACHES

ACRYLICS

OILS

Paints old and new
Many paints have unusual names. They are often named after the plant, rock, earth, animal, or place they come from. See how adding a little white paint affects each colour.

Using oil paints

If you use oil paints, you will need these special liquids:

Turpentine (turps) or white spirit
These are used to clean brushes. They are poisonous.

Linseed oil
This is mixed with oil paint to make it more runny.

Painter's equipment

Have these things ready before you start to paint:

Water
Water is mixed with all paints except oils. Always keep your water clean.

Rags
These are important. Always wash and dry your brushes before using a new colour.

Palettes
You can mix paint on palettes and saucers.

Apron
Wear an apron or old shirt to protect your clothes.

Tools, brushes, and papers

There are many ways of applying paint, and a wide variety of surfaces to work on. You will need different brushes and papers depending on the type of paint you use.

Brushes

Take time to choose your brushes and try to build up a collection of different ones (the numbers on the brushes show their size and thickness). Experiment with all the marks that brushes can make – large sweeps, short dabs, flat washes, dry smudges, strokes in all directions, curly and straight. Below is a typical selection of brushes that you might like to try.

Paper

The type of paper you use can have an effect on the end result of your painting. Try out thin and thick, coloured and fine, rough and handmade papers, but avoid shiny paper as wet paint slides off its surface. Watercolour paint needs special, slightly rougher paper to hold the paint. Decorator's lining paper is good for large, bold paintings.

A selection of brushes

Flat brush

Filbert brush

Round brush

Bright brush

Chinese brush for use with inks

Good brush with evenly fat bristles

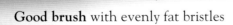

Bad brush with spluttery hairs

A selection of papers

Brown paper

Rice paper

Blue sugar paper

Red cartridge paper

Watercolour paper

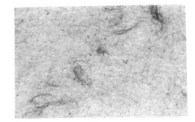

Handmade paper

Useful painting tools

Sponge
Use a sponge to blot up watercolour paint or to apply thick paint.

Decorating roller
Small rollers are good for applying broad sweeps of colour.

Decorating brush
Good for large-scale paintings using acrylic paints and housepaints.

Taking care of your brushes

Try not to leave your brushes standing in water or turps for too long or the bristles will lose their shape. Make sure they are clean after use.

A painter's canvas

Most oil paintings are painted on a canvas. This is usually a piece of linen cloth that has been stretched over a frame or board and then protected with primer (paint).

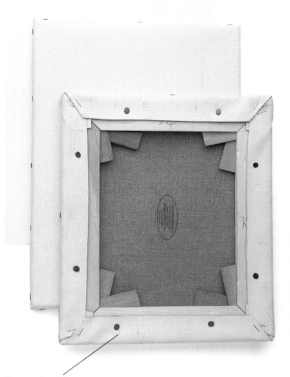

Stretched canvas
This is the back of a canvas. The linen has been pulled tight and tacked down on a wooden frame called a stretcher.

Your studio
Make sure you have good light and plenty of space before you start to paint. If you don't have an easel, a table or the floor will do instead.

The painter's studio
This photograph of the English painter Frank Auerbach's studio shows us one of his oil paintings in progress, with thick brushes and pots of oil paint to hand. A photograph of a friend's painting is on the wall.

Easel
A large easel holds the painting. The handle is used to change the easel's height.

Sketches
Most of the sketches on the wall and in the sketchbook are ideas for the painting.

Newspaper
Cover the floor or table where you are working with newspaper.

Water
Keep your water to the left of your paper if you are left-handed, and to the right if right-handed.

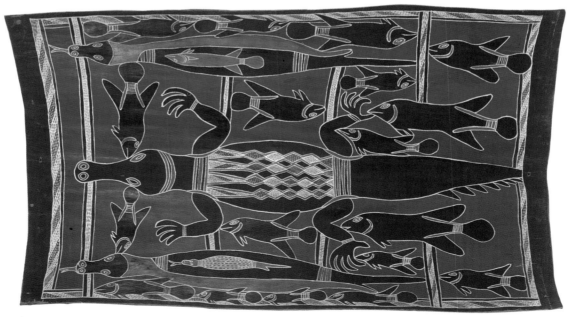

MUTIPUY OF THE DJAPU TRIBE *Title unknown* 1973

The Australian Aboriginal artist Mutipuy of the Djapu Tribe painted this picture of fish and crocodiles on bark. Many modern Aboriginal artists still use bark to paint on in the traditional way. Their paintings are almost always about the land and their ancestors. Here Mutipuy has made a painting about his religious ancestor, the crocodile.

The world of colour

Pure, vivid colour is an exciting part of our world. In nature, fruit, flowers, rainbows, tropical fish, and birds attract our attention with their brilliance. People use colour to catch our eye, too – think of clothes, traffic lights, and advertisements. Mixing colours to make the exact shade you want is one of the most important skills a painter can learn. Did you know that you can make most colours with just red, yellow, and blue paints?

The colour wheel

The colour wheel is a diagram that helps us to understand more about colours and how they affect one another. Red, yellow, and blue are called primary colours because they cannot be made from any other colours. Orange, green, and purple are called secondary colours because they are made by mixing two primary colours together.

Secondary colours
Each secondary colour – green, orange, and purple – is a mixture of the two primary colours next to it on the wheel.

Primary colours
Yellow, red, and blue are primary colours.

Making secondary colours

Secondary shades
You can make many shades of orange by mixing different amounts of red and yellow together.

Try making a secondary colour by mixing two primary colours together. Clean your brush and dry it on a paper tissue or rag every time you mix a new colour.

Complementary colours
The complementary pairs of colours are red and green, orange and blue, and yellow and purple.

Complementary and harmonizing colours

Each colour of the colour wheel has a complementary colour, which sits opposite it on the wheel. When two complementary colours are put side by side, they contrast with each other and seem more vivid. Colours that share a pigment, such as blue and green, are called harmonizing colours, because when they are put side by side, they appear to blend together.

Side by side
Look at these three pairs of colours. The same orange colour was blobbed in the middle of rings of blue, red, and yellow paint. In which ring does the orange look brightest. Why is this?

EDWARD LEAR *The Red and Yellow Macaw 1831*
In this watercolour sketch, you can see how the English artist and comic writer Edward Lear has made a detailed study of the macaw and has tried to mix his paints to match the bright colours of its feathers.

ANDRÉ DERAIN *Boats in the Port of Collioure 1905*

In this painting, the French artist Derain used primary and secondary colours to express the heat and bright sunlight in a fishing port in the South of France, rather than matching the colours he actually saw. People were so shocked by these unnatural colours, that they nicknamed Derain and other French artists who painted in this way "Fauves", which means "Wild Beasts".

Exploring colours

Collect a few objects in each of the colours of the colour wheel. Arrange them together and look at the different ways colours affect one another. Have you put any complementary or harmonizing colours together?

Colour contrasts

The iris has purple and yellow petals. Can you see any other pairs of complementary colours in this arrangement?

Colour harmony

Try arranging your objects so that all the harmonizing colours are together. Then see if you can mix paints to match the different shades.

Painting a still-life

Paint your favourite arrangement of objects, filling the paper with colour, right up to the edge. Mix plenty of paint and try to match the colours of the objects as accurately as you can.

Colour and light

The more you paint and observe, the more you will realize that the actual colours you see depend on the amount of light falling on them. Try putting a brightly coloured object near a window. Can you see that it becomes split into areas of light and shadow, changing the colour that you see? These slight changes of colour are called tones. There are many ways of painting light and shadow: here are some for you to try.

Light lightens
A colour is lightest where most light falls on it.

Look inside
Here the light falls on the inside of the jug, showing that it is hollow.

Middle tone
The middle tone is the tone closest to the actual colour of the jug.

Curving round
The changes of light on the jug show us that it is round and hollow.

Dark shadow
A colour is darkest where least light falls on it.

Paint the colours that you see
You can try mixing colours to make lighter and darker tones. But first, you will need to mix a colour to match the middle tone of your object.

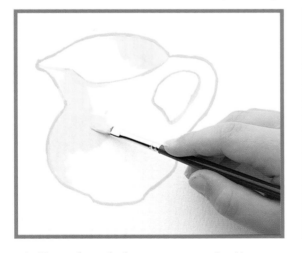

1 To make a lighter tone, gradually mix some white paint with your middle tone. When it matches the light tone you see, add the lighter tone to your painting.

2 To make a darker tone of the middle colour, gradually mix in a little of its complementary colour until it matches the dark tone you see.

Daylight colours
This plain yellow jug has been placed beside a window with its lip pointing towards the light. Look at the areas of light and shadow and the tones of colour that have appeared on its rounded surface.

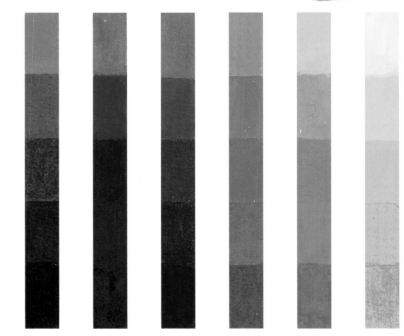

Tone down
A little purple added to yellow makes a darker tone of yellow.

The tone ladder
Here is a series of tone ladders which shows lighter and darker tones of each of the colours on the colour wheel. One way of making light or dark tones of a colour is by adding increasing amounts of white or of its complementary colour (not too much, though). Recognizing tones may take time, but the game below can help you practise.

Tone ladder game
Try finding the lightest green on the ladder, then find its match in tone on the other colour ladders. Play the game by matching as many tones as you can.

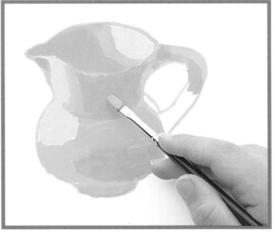

✍ Complementary shadows

See how Renoir has used blue and its complementary colour, orange, to create the shadowed path in his painting called *The Swing*, on the right.

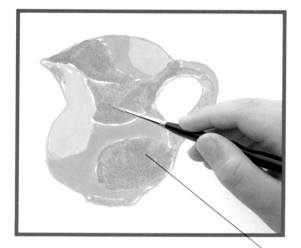

No-mix shadows

Try painting your object again, this time using just the complementary colour for the darker areas. You could also try this when you paint light and shadow outside, as Renoir did.

Tone tips

Try to use a tone of the complementary colour that is as close as possible to the tone of your middle colour. Use the tone ladder to help.

Side by side

Purple is placed next to the yellow and not mixed with it, to create the dark tone.

PIERRE AUGUSTE RENOIR *The Swing* 1876

Renoir was one of the group of 19th-century French painters known as the Impressionists. By painting outside, they observed the changes of light and colour in nature. They chose to use complementary colours to show shadows (instead of blacks and browns) as a way of filling their paintings with light and colour.

GEORGES SEURAT *The Circus Parade* 1887-8

Georges Seurat was a French painter who was influenced by the Impressionists, but who also developed his own colour theories. He is known as a Pointillist because instead of mixing his colours on the palette, he kept them separate in tiny dots (points) on the canvas. See how the effect of bright artificial light behind the trombone player is created by using many different coloured dots.

✍ Optical mixing

Seurat's method of painting is called optical mixing because the separate dots merge to create a new colour in the viewer's eye, rather than on the painter's palette. Experiment with creating light and dark colours by placing tiny dots of colour side by side.

Dotty detail

Look at this detail of a shadowed area in the painting. By using light dots of paint, as well as dark, Seurat has made even the darkest areas glow with colour.

Earth-colours

Look at the clouds, at mud, at bricks, at wood, and at stone, and think about how you would mix all the different blacks, greys, and browns that you see. You may have ready-mixed brown, grey, and black in your paint set, but if you wish to capture the variety of these natural colours in paint, you will need to experiment further with mixing the colours of the colour wheel and making light and dark tones.

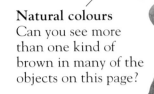

Natural colours
Can you see more than one kind of brown in many of the objects on this page?

Similar colours
Does this colour remind you of the dress worn by Velazquez's princess?

Mixing earth-colours

1 Try mixing all three primary colours together on a saucer. What happens if you change the amount of each of the colours you use?

2 See how many kinds of brown you can make by mixing any two secondary colours together.

3 Try mixing all the primary and secondary colours together to make black (don't use too much yellow). If you add small amounts of white paint, how many tones of grey can you mix?

ALBERT PINKHAM RYDER *Jonah c.1885*

The American artist Ryder used light and dark earth-colours to make his painting of the Bible story of Jonah and the whale look wild and stormy. Look at the way he swirled colours together to express the dramatic movement of the sea and sky.

✏️ Collecting colours

Collect all sorts of grey, brown, black, and white objects from inside and outdoors. Look for a variety of tones – mousy browns, smoky greys, chestnut, and raven black – like the ones on this page. Then try the paint-mixing experiment below.

Mix and match
Check the colour you have mixed by blobbing paint beside the object you are matching.

Subtle colours
See how this colour is almost halfway between brown and grey.

Spicy brown
See if you can mix the rich, dark brown of this star anise.

Paler colours
Try adding a little white paint to make pale tones.

DIEGO RODRIGUEZ DA SILVA Y VELAZQUEZ
Maria Teresa de Espagna 1652

The Spanish artist Velazquez used just a few earth-colours to paint this richly coloured portrait of a Spanish princess. Look at the way the artist added a warm coral colour for the decorations on her dress and in her hair. See how this contrasts with the other colours in the painting.

Matching earth-colours

1 Mix colours to match each of your objects and put strokes of these colours on a sheet of paper. Fill the page with blobs, splodges, and thick and thin strokes of each of the colours you mix.

2 When the page is full, see if you can turn the blob-covered paper into a painting of a person, an animal, or a landscape. Try adding a primary colour to contrast with the earth-colours, or use black and white lines to complete your picture.

Colour and feelings

How do the various colours on your palette make you feel? Are there some colours that you associate with happy feelings, and some with sad? We think of red, orange, and yellow as warm colours because they are linked to fire and sunlight; while blues, greys, and violets seem cold like ice, or cool and fresh like the sky. Experiment and you will gradually discover your own ways of using colour to express the mood or subject of your painting.

Painting colour-washes

Wet some small sheets of watercolour or blotting paper under the tap, then mix a broad range of colours and tones in watercolour. Use a large brush to sweep two different colour-washes across the paper and up to the edges, letting the colours merge and make shapes.

Colour combinations

Pin up your paintings and take time to decide how each coloured sheet makes you feel. Give them titles based on your feelings, such as anger, joy, fear, or love.

Warm colours

Cool colours

Warm and cool colours

MARK ROTHKO *No. 12 1951*

The American painter Mark Rothko was part of a group of 20th-century artists known as Abstract Expressionists. These artists wanted to find a way of painting that did not use scenes from real life, but instead expressed moods and feelings. In this large painting, Rothko paints colours that seem to hover in front of the canvas. How does this painting make you feel?

Complementary colours

Painting game

Choose one word from each of the sections below, then paint a picture using colour to express the word from the "feelings" section. Below you can see three children's paintings that were inspired by this game.

FEELINGS	sad angry happy friendly anxious frightened mysterious peaceful envious heroic
CHARACTERS	cat child soldier dancer old lady magician traveller spectre horse
PLACES	sea castle forest desert a room mountains garden circus river road
CONDITIONS	sun rain wind evening burning heat night-time storm dawn snow

EMIL NOLDE *The Last Supper 1909*

The German artist Nolde used colour to help express his deep religious feelings in this painting of the Last Supper. Here Jesus is telling his disciples that one of them will betray him to the Romans. Notice the blood red colours, which contrast harshly with the bright green, and look at the bitter yellow of the faces and at Christ's pure white robe.

HENRY (aged 10) *Riding in the Mountains 1993*
Heroic • horse • mountains • evening

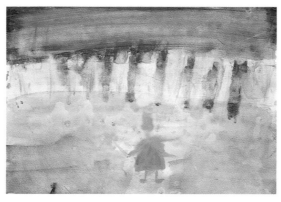

JO (aged 10) *Magician 1993*
Mysterious • magician • forest • rain

WILLIAM (aged 9) *Desert Traveller 1993*
Peaceful • traveller • desert • evening

Sketching ideas

A sketch is a quick drawing or painting that gives a rough idea of something you have seen, felt, or imagined. Many artists carry a sketchbook around with them all the time to explore ideas for paintings and to record things that interest them. You can use your sketchbook to make studies from nature, from paintings that you like in art galleries, or to invent subjects from your imagination. Picasso wrote on one of his sketchbooks, "I am my sketchbook", as if it were a visual diary of his life.

Using a sketchbook

Portable size
It is a good idea to have a pocket-sized sketchbook that you can carry about.

Keeping a "diary"
Never throw away your sketchbooks. Keep them for reference.

Watercolour pencils
If you go over your sketch with a wet brush, you can create the effect of watercolours.

Sketching materials
Try sketching in a range of different materials.

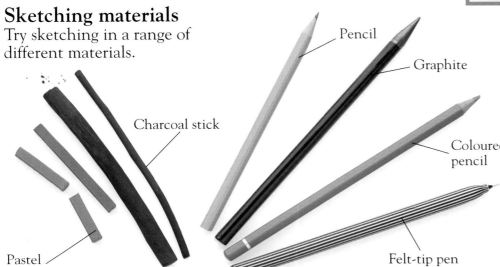

Pencil

Graphite

Charcoal stick

Coloured pencil

Pastel

Felt-tip pen

Rubber

Putty rubber

Pencil sharpener

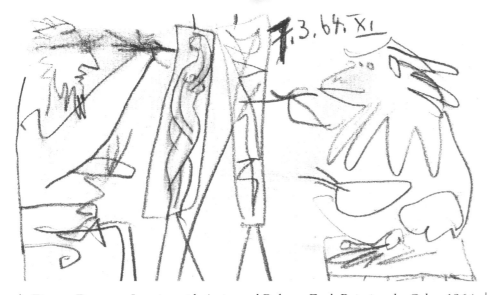

PABLO PICASSO *Interior with Artist and Baboon Each Painting the Other 1964*

By experimenting in his many sketchbooks, the Spanish artist Picasso developed serious and funny ideas for his paintings. In this pencil sketch, he has transformed a few squiggly pencil lines into a baboon and an artist painting each other at their easels. What do you think Picasso is saying about art?

LEONARDO DA VINCI *Studies of a Dragon Fight 1511*

The Italian artist and inventor Leonardo da Vinci used his sketchbooks to make detailed drawings from nature and his imagination, and of ideas for inventions. He often added notes in mirror-writing.

Imagination game

Artists have always enjoyed using their imagination to discover shapes in doodles. You can play this game on your own or with a friend, making scribbles for each other.

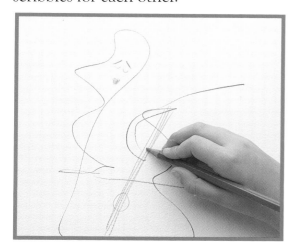

Shut your eyes and make a scribble on some paper without thinking about it. Turn the paper around until you see something emerging from the lines and transform it into your imagined subject.

Sketching tools

Experiment with the different effects you can create by sketching in felt-tip pen, pastel, and charcoal.

PEGGY SOMERVILLE *Spring Shower 1928*

This charcoal sketch was made by the English artist Peggy Somerville when she was only ten years old. Look at the way she has used the charcoal very quickly with many different marks to give the impression of a sudden spring shower as it blows across the landscape. She usually conjured up such sketches from her imagination.

Rubber drawing
You can use your putty rubber to draw white lines on areas of charcoal.

Coloured pastels

You can use coloured pastels or pencils to make a study of the light and colour of a subject in preparation for a painting.

Nature in detail
It is surprising how much you can see if you study something closely.

Felt-tip pen

A fine felt-tip pen is good for doing small, detailed studies of a subject because you can make thin lines that do not smudge.

Changing nature
You can capture passing moments such as this evening light with pastels.

Charcoal

Charcoal is soft and moves quickly over paper, so it is useful for larger sketches. You can make a variety of black marks and shapes, or smudge it to create atmosphere with your fingers or a putty rubber.

Shape

A shape can be made by finding the line that seems to go around the edge of something. Everything has its own shape, which helps us to recognize what it is. Shapes can be expressive – some are curvy and friendly, while others seem spiky and wicked. We all think we know the shape of a cat, but if we look closely at one particular cat and the way it is sitting, we will find that it makes its own special shape. Think about what you like about certain shapes and arrange them in your painting in a way that pleases you.

What is this shape?

Sometimes the most familiar animal can make a shape that is hard to recognize.

All is revealed
Can you see how the shapes of the two front legs have combined to make one shape? Does this happen anywhere else?

Discover animal shapes

Investigate the shape of a familiar animal. Observe your subject carefully, starting with its most recognizable viewpoint.

Finding shapes
It may help when drawing a shape to imagine circles, triangles, squares, or rectangles on top of the shape of your animal.

PIERRE BONNARD *Two Dogs 1891*

The French painter Bonnard was very curious about shapes and enjoyed arranging them in his paintings. Here you can see that he was interested in the shape between the playing dogs (the negative shape), as well as the outline of the dogs themselves. This could also be a painting of a sea and two islands! How many circle shapes can you find in this painting?

Posing pets
Find poses that you like and that seem typical of your animal.

Painting animal shapes

1 Draw the outline of your animal. Sometimes the shape may seem very strange, but keep going. (If you make a mistake, just leave it and draw a new line in the right place.)

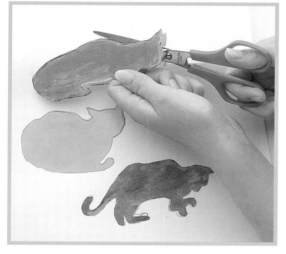

2 Draw your animal from two more viewpoints and paint each shape in a different colour. Cut out your shapes and then arrange them on a piece of coloured paper so that they tell a story.

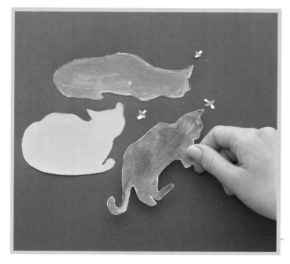

3 When you are arranging the shapes, think about the negative shape you create between them, then stick them down. You can try adding extra shapes, such as these bees, to complete your story.

MANOHAR DAS *The Young Manohar and the Scribe 1581*

This Indian miniature contains a self-portrait of the artist (the figure kneeling on the left), who painted it when he was just 15 years old. Look at the different shapes in the painting. See how the artist has used rich colours to emphasize the shapes and has made them appear quite flat.

Different shapes In this diagram, the red lines show some curvy shapes and the green lines show some straight shapes. See how they fit together in the painting.

Echoing shapes See how the curvy red shapes echo each other in the painting.

Combining shapes in your paintings

Look out for things that have similar shapes. For example, the elephant's trunk below is rather like a teapot's spout. Create a painting in which you place an animal of your choice with other interesting shapes.

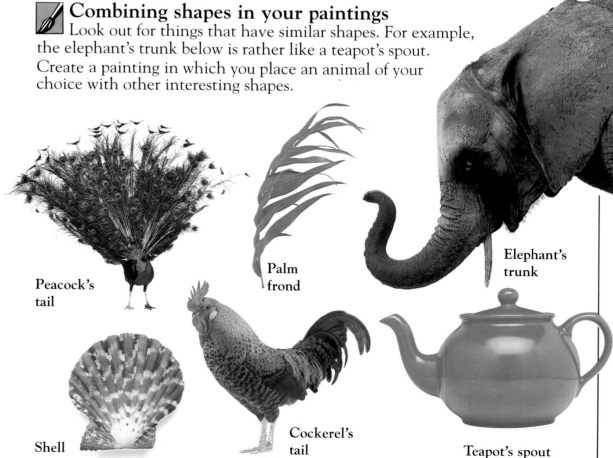

Peacock's tail

Palm frond

Elephant's trunk

Shell

Cockerel's tail

Teapot's spout

Pattern

If a shape, or a group of shapes, is repeated a number of times in a painting, it creates a pattern. In your paintings, you may enjoy experimenting with a number of similar and contrasting patterns and combining them in different ways. Try painting the patterns you see, or create an abstract painting that is all about pattern.

Painting patterns
Look for an object that has an interesting pattern. Study it closely and draw what you see, using a pencil.

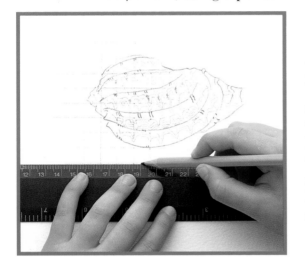

1 Choose a part of your pattern to enlarge. You could try enlarging this part freely, or else draw a grid over the pattern to help you enlarge it bit by bit.

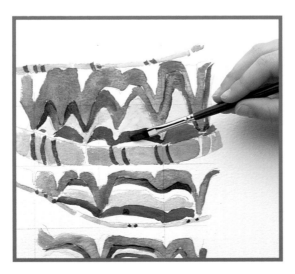

2 Enlarge your pattern to cover the whole paper. (If you have used a grid, enlarge this first.) Paint your pattern, repeating the colours when the shapes repeat. Enjoy your abstract painting.

Pattern hunt
You can see patterns everywhere if you look for them – in natural objects like shells and flowers, as well as in tiles, fabrics, and many household objects. How many can you find around your home?

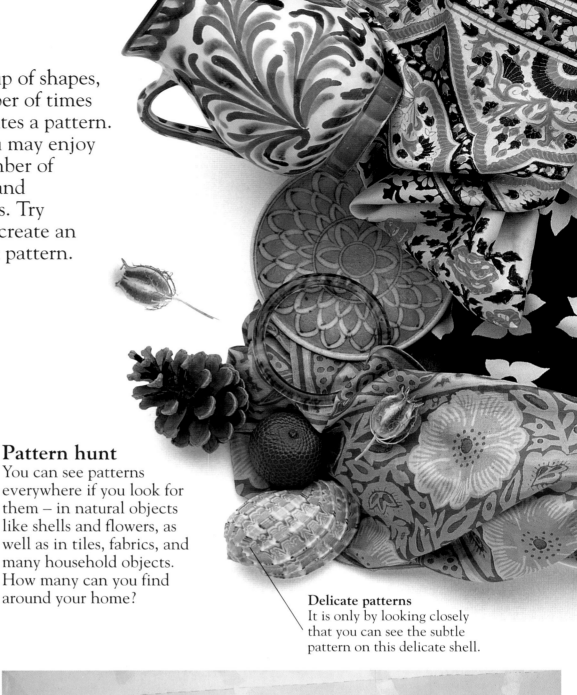

Delicate patterns
It is only by looking closely that you can see the subtle pattern on this delicate shell.

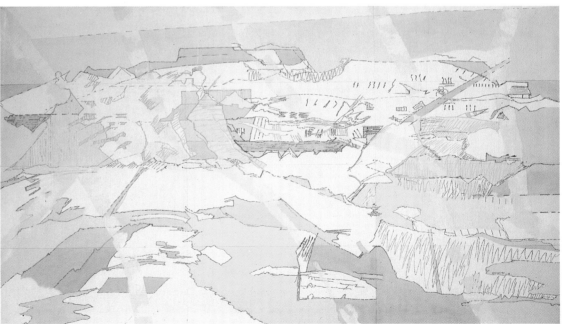

FLAVIA IRWIN *Geomorphological Exploits III 1992*

The British artist Irwin enjoys studying patterns she sees in the landscape. She makes a drawing, on the spot, of fields and hedges, then enlarges her image freely on to a canvas. She finds delicate colours to create an abstract painting about pattern and shape.

✎ Patterns in art

Patterns are used in many art forms to decorate the surface of objects and to attract attention. Paint a combination of patterned materials and objects that you find around you.

Contrasting patterns
This large pattern contrasts with the smaller ones.

Animal patterns
Which animal does this pattern remind you of?

EDOUARD VUILLARD *Woman in Blue with a Child* c.1899

The French artist Vuillard uses many dense patterns and strong shapes in this family scene. See how the patterns of fabric and wallpaper invite us to look more slowly at the painting. The mother and child are hidden in the pattern and it takes time to discover a cat lying on the bed.

Irregular patterns
Look at the strange irregular pattern made by the craters in this dried lotus flower seed-head.

Aerial photograph of fields

Sometimes you can only see underlying patterns at a distance. This photograph of fields was taken from the air. Can you see smaller patterns within the larger patterns?

Similar patterns
The patterns in this area are so alike that it is hard to see the separate objects.

✎ Patterns in nature

Patterns are essential to the survival of many birds and animals, disguising them from their enemies or their prey. Create a painting in which a wild animal or bird is camouflaged in its natural habitat.

Rhythm and movement

Sometimes you may want to paint subjects that are moving such as animals, dancers, or athletes. In nature, trees bend in the wind, waves roll, and clouds scud across the sky. How do you create a sense of movement on the flat, still surface of a painting? Painters use lines and shapes to lead our eyes in different directions. Vertical and horizontal lines seem still and steady, while curved or diagonal lines lean over, giving the impression of movement.

Capturing movement

Still boat
If the boat is painted using vertical and horizontal lines, it appears to be still in a calm sea.

Moving boat
Here the boat is diagonal and the waves are leaning and curved, giving a sense of rhythm and movement.

Feeling steady
Try standing upright with your feet firmly planted and feel how still and steady you are.

Stand still
The cloth hangs still and straight.

On the move
When you move, it is impossible to keep all parts of your body vertical.

Floating
Here the cloth makes a curving, flowing shape.

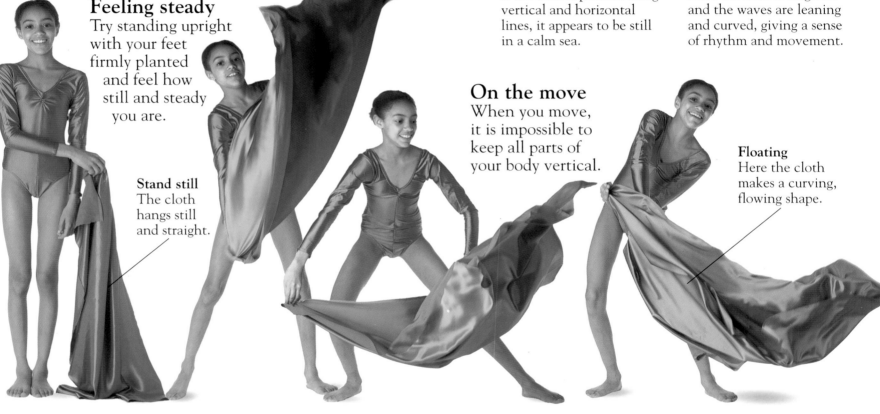

ROSA BONHEUR *The Horse Fair* 1853–5

This painting by the 19th-century French artist Bonheur was one of the most popular pictures of its day. It celebrates the power and energy of thundering horses and in real life this painting is very large. See how the light and dark colours make your eyes flicker across the painting, creating movement.

Lines of movement
The diagram below helps us to see the underlying diagonal and curving lines that give Bonheur's painting rhythm and movement. The red diagonal lines seem to pull against the green ones, like the grooms reining in the horses.

Still, steady lines
Look at the line of vertical trees and the church, and see how their stillness makes us even more aware of the movement of the animals.

Diagonals
Each olive tree leans in the same direction. As the trees become smaller, they create a diagonal across the painting.

Swirls
Swirling brushmarks exaggerate the curved branches of the trees, which have become twisted by strong winds over many years.

VINCENT VAN GOGH *The Apilles with Olive Trees in the Foreground 1889*

The 19th-century Dutch artist van Gogh painted this landscape in the South of France. He was attracted by the strong shapes and ancient olive trees. See how van Gogh has filled his painting with rhythm and movement. Like Rosa Bonheur's horses, everything appears to be galloping across the canvas.

Moving images
Look at the Bonheur and van Gogh paintings on these pages. Choose a subject that is full of movement and create a painting that combines diagonals, curves, and swirling brushstrokes. It is a good idea to plot out the lines of movement before you start.

Rhythm
Repeated curves and colours set up a rhythm as if the figure is dancing to music.

Leaping and leaning
Like the curves of the billowing cloth, the dancer's body curves and leans as she leaps in the air.

Flickering colours
Using a variety of light and dark colours encourages your eyes to skip around the painting from one patch of colour to another.

Speed
Unfinished, sketchy brushstrokes can give the impression that they have been done in a hurry to catch the movement in a subject.

Brushstrokes
Separate brushstrokes, flowing in the same direction, swirl like the current of a river. Try creating curls and spirals too.

Technique and texture

What other tools and objects can you paint with, apart from a brush? Look for things around your home that could be used to create textures and patterns. Move around a large piece of paper on the (newspaper-covered) floor, and try using a variety of marks and gestures to make an abstract painting. Experiment with thick and thin paint. Can you invent new techniques and effects of your own?

Dabbing
Try a toothbrush for short dabs.

Blowing
A blob of thin paint can be blown across the paper with a drinking-straw.

Thickening paint

Thick paint will add texture to your painting. Water-based paints can be thickened with PVA glue.

Rolling
A decorating roller can be used to make long sweeping marks.

Dripping
Drip paint randomly across the paper from a yoghurt pot with a small hole in the bottom.

1 You can buy ready-mixed, water-based paints in large, squeezy bottles. These are good for painting a large picture. Find a bowl in which you can mix the glue and paint.

2 Put some ready-mixed paint into the bowl and then add the PVA glue in small amounts. Stir the glue in until you have just the thickness of paint you want.

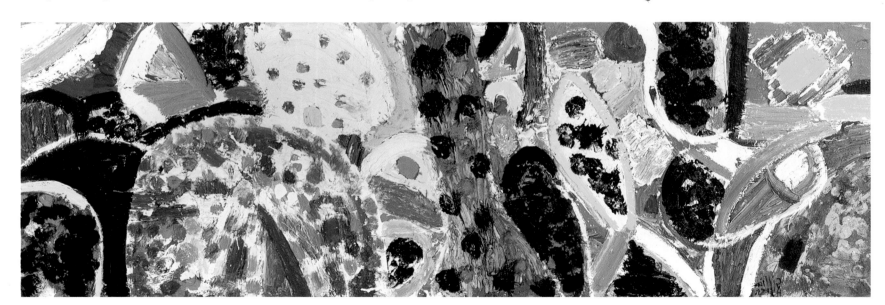

GILLIAN AYRES *Salix* 1991

The English artist Ayres uses very thick paint and brilliant colours for her highly textured paintings. The paint is so thick that it stands out from the canvas. *Salix* means "willow" – which gives us a clue to the theme of the painting. Can you see a fish and a waterlily leaf?

Marks and gestures
Thick strokes, short dabs, round blobs, and broad patches all go in different directions, creating a fascinating surface.

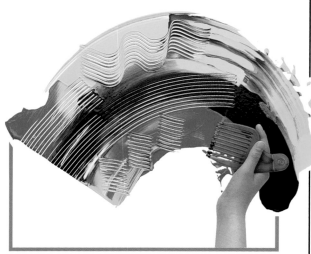

Combing

Use different objects to make patterns of thick and thin lines in the paint. A piece of card is good for spreading a big blob of paint smoothly on to the paper. Use an old comb, or another tool, to make marks in the paint.

Brushing and flicking

Experiment with a big decorating brush. You need to have quite a lot of paint ready for this. Try flicking paint on to the paper with a smaller brush.

SHARON PETERS *Farewell 1993*

Action painting

Put some action into your painting by using fingers, hands, and feet to make marks. You can even run across your painting if you like.

Squirting and dribbling

Half-fill an empty washing-up liquid bottle with runny paint (with the help of a funnel). Dribble thin lines and marks, or try squeezing and squirting the paint.

Sponging

Use a sponge for making soft, smudgy effects and shapes. Experiment with using different amounts of paint on your sponge.

Painting solid forms

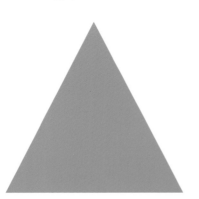 Solid form is the three-dimensional shape of an object. People, houses, mountains, and fruit – most things in our world – are not flat but three-dimensional, like a sculpture. If you are making a sculpture, you can model your subject from all sides, but you cannot do this in a flat painting. Instead, you have to look at the way that light falls across something, showing you its solid form and what it is made of.

C.E. BROCK *Illustration from Gulliver's Travels 1894*
This scene from Jonathan Swift's story can help you think about solid form. Gulliver's body seems like a three-dimensional mountain to the tiny Lilliputian figures scrambling over him.

Flat and solid
Which of these two shapes is the solid, three-dimensional one? The answer is neither! If you run your finger across the shapes on the page, you will find that they are both flat, but the pyramid, with its shadows, just looks solid.

Thinking solid
When you paint lumpy, solid forms, imagine your paintbrush is a Lilliputian or an explorer walking over sunlit mountains and down into dark, shadowed valleys.

Shadowy faces
Ask a friend, or one of your family, to sit for you near a lamp. Make sure the light is placed so that the lumps and bumps on the face are highlighted, and the dips are in deep shadow.

GEORGES DE LA TOUR *The Cheat with the Ace of Diamonds (date unknown)*

The 17th-century French painter Georges de la Tour was fascinated by the way artificial light (candles in those days) could illuminate solid forms, creating mysterious shadows and atmosphere. How has the artist used sharp contrasts of light and shadow to pick out the "shady" character (the cheat) in this game of cards? Can you imagine what the other players are thinking?

White on black
See if you can paint the "lumps" of the face using a light-coloured paint on a piece of dark paper. You will soon see its solid form emerge.

Paintings or photographs

After photography was invented in 1839, some painters decided they could leave detailed, realistic copying to the camera. They felt free to explore new ways of making their subjects look real and solid.

LILLY (aged 9)
Bowl of Fruit
1993

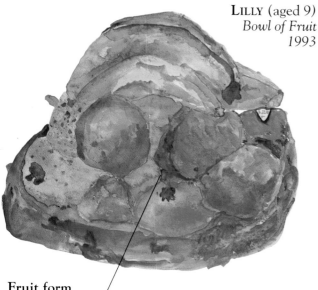

Fruit form
See how different this watercolour is from a photograph, and how well the paint shows the beauty of the fruit.

PAUL CÉZANNE *Still-life with Apples, a Bottle, and a Milk Pot 1902-6*

The 19th-century French painter Cézanne found his own way of painting people, nature, and still-lifes so that they looked real and solid. In this watercolour, he uses brushmarks and changes of colour to show the play of bright light on the objects. Notice how Cézanne uses complementary colours for some of the shadows.

A solid still-life

Arrange a still-life of fruit and other objects on a table where daylight falls across them. Paint a watercolour of your set-up on white watercolour paper. Try and find a way to make your painting show how solid the objects really are.

Weighing up your objects
Hold an apple in your hand to feel its weight and volume. Turn it around to feel its individual form.

Watercolour whites
Here are some of the ways you can put white highlights in your watercolour paintings. You can either leave parts of the paper white (as Cézanne has done), use a sponge to lift off some of the paint, or add a little white gouache to the paint.

White paper

White gouache

Sponge

Seeing shapes
It often helps to imagine a simple three-dimensional structure such as a pyramid, a sphere, or a cylinder inside the object you are painting.

Colour from front to back
Look at the variety of colours in one apple. Start painting the part of the apple nearest to you, then, using dabs of colour, work your way around towards the back of its form.

Front and back
Think about the back of each object, even though you cannot see it.

Painting people

H ave you ever tried to paint people as you really see them? If you look closely you will discover that no two people have exactly the same shaped face, skin colour, proportions, or even way of sitting. In order to paint life-like people, you will also need to remember that they are solid forms and individuals full of character.

Eyes
How far down the head are the eyes? Do both eyes look exactly the same? Do the eyelids cover part of the iris?

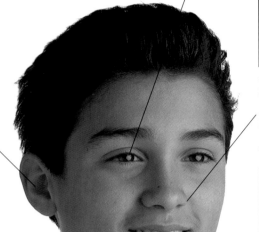

Ears
Where are the ears in relation to the eyes? (Can you even see the ears?)

Nose
Where do the nostrils come between the eyes and the chin?

Mouth
Look at the shape of the mouth. It shows a person's character well.

Painting faces
Paint the head and shoulders slightly turned to one side. Stand close by and keep the same viewpoint.

Whole head
Paint the solid form of the head and shoulders before the details of the face.

Painting figures
Now try to paint the whole figure, seated and facing slightly to the left or right. This time you will need to stand further away so that you can see all of your subject. Remember to keep the same viewpoint while you are painting.

Whole body
Map out the whole figure first.

Measuring proportions

When you are painting, you can get an idea of the size of one part of a figure compared with another part by using this simple trick:

Keep your arm straight and hold your brush upright or level, depending on whether you want to measure downwards or across. Close one eye and find the height of the hair, for example, marking it with your thumb on the paintbrush. Check this measurement against that of another part of the body.

Measuring height   Measuring width

Head
What size is the head when compared to the rest of the body?

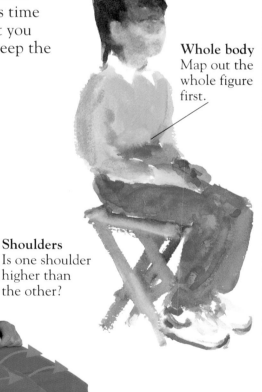

Halfway line
Imagine a horizontal line halfway down your figure. Whereabouts on your subject is this line ?

Shoulders
Is one shoulder higher than the other?

Pose and form
Look at how your friend is sitting and imagine the solid weight of the body on the chair.

The background
Sketch in the floor and walls around your figure, or it will seem to float in mid-air.

Foreshortening
Sometimes the way a person is sitting looks odd. This girl's foot is nearer to you so it looks much larger. The rest of the leg seems squashed up. This illusion is called foreshortening.

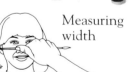

TOMMASO MASACCIO AND FILIPPO LIPPI *The Resurrection of Theophilus' Son (detail)* *c.1428*

This detail is just one part of a large painting on the walls of the Brancacci Chapel in Florence, Italy, that shows crowds of people witnessing a miracle. It was painted on wet plaster (fresco) nearly 600 years ago by Masaccio and Lippi. The artists were famous for making people seem real and solid by showing the light and shadow on their faces.

Different faces
Look at the way the artists have captured the individual characters through different skin colours and the variety of noses, mouths, and eyes.

Moving figures

A moving figure changes position constantly. Observe and sketch people moving, or look at figures in photographs. Notice the angles of people's bodies as they do different things and the shapes their bodies make. Paint your observations and use them in your pictures.

MARY CASSATT *Young Mother Sewing 1902*

In this painting, the American artist Cassatt captures a moment of family life, with the light pouring through a window onto the figures and a vase of flowers. The loose brush marks describe the clothes, the folds of which show the form of the bodies underneath. See how natural the mother's and the child's hands are.

Side views
The left side of this running figure is mainly hidden by the right.

Clothes
Folds of clothes can show the solid form of the body underneath.

Diagonals
When running, the body leans forward, creating diagonal lines.

Space

Have you noticed that the more space there is between you and an object the smaller it looks, while the closer it is the bigger it seems? You may also notice that when something is nearer to you, it may hide or overlap things further back. Try using these two observations when you paint, to make your pictures look more real and three-dimensional.

Putting people in the picture

These figures appear to be the same size because they are standing side by side.

What happens if one person steps towards you and the others move further away?

Overlapping
Closer figures hide parts of the figures behind them.

Far people
The girl's hand and the smallest figure seem to be almost the same size.

Near and far
See for yourself how figures look smaller in the distance. Hold up your hand and compare its size with the sizes of people standing nearby and far away. Do any of the figures overlap?

Painting real space
De Witte uses changing size and overlapping of objects to help give the illusion of real space.

EMMANUEL DE WITTE *Interior with a Woman at a Clavichord c.1665*

The 17th-century Dutch painter de Witte uses fascinating tricks to make us think that we are looking into real space. It is hard to believe that you cannot walk into this peaceful room, past the woman playing the clavichord, and on through three rooms to look out of the open window at the end. The light flooding in from the windows on the right creates a pattern that leads your eye into the distance.

Size
Compare the doorways and see how they grow smaller, the deeper into space they are.

Overlapping
This woman hides the clavichord so we know she must be in front of it. Can you find other overlaps?

City space

Cities are dramatic spaces, particularly when viewed from high up. The cars and people seem very small because they are far away.

Going into the distance
See how the street and the buildings seem to shrink as they disappear into the distance.

Creating space

It is quite difficult to create a feeling of space and distance in a painting, so try cutting out and arranging images first, then try to use the ideas in your paintings.

GEORGE GROSZ *The Big City* 1916-17

In this painting, the 20th-century German artist Grosz has used space in an imaginative way to express his own frightening vision of modern city life. Diagonal, rushing figures, speeding trams, and huge buildings come surging toward you, and the space is very crowded. See how the figures overlap, and compare the sizes of the close and the distant people.

1 Choose a playground, city square, or market as your subject. Paint lots of images relating to your theme such as figures, animals, cars, and buses, in three different sizes. They can be as life-like and detailed, or as simple as you wish.

2 Cut out your figures and sort them into three groups according to size – small, medium, or large. Paint the playground, square, or market (without any people) on a small sheet of paper. Make this space quite simple.

3 Arrange the small figures at the top of the paper, and glue them down firmly. Overlap these with medium figures, then glue them down. Finally, arrange, and then glue the large figures at the bottom.

Composition

Composition is the arrangement of the different parts of your painting. It is the way in which you organize colours, shapes, forms, lines, and brushmarks to tell the story of your painting, or what you like about its subject. Composing a picture includes choosing its shape and size, deciding what to put in it and what to leave out, choosing and arranging colours, and creating the impression of space. Look at the artists' paintings in this book – can you tell at a glance what each painting is about, just by its composition?

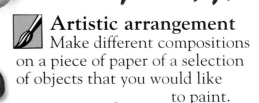

Artistic arrangement
Make different compositions on a piece of paper of a selection of objects that you would like to paint.

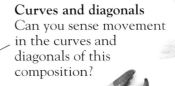

Composing an image
A painting can be any size or shape, depending on what you want to show about your subject. If you arrange a group of objects in several ways, you will create some very different images.

Curves and diagonals
Can you sense movement in the curves and diagonals of this composition?

Different formats
Notice how the shape of the picture (format) seems to suggest the arrangement.

Shapes and textures
Can you see how similar shapes and textures have been grouped together in blocks? Compare this with the other composition.

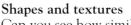

ELIZABETH BLACKADDER *Still-life, Bamboo and Gold 1991*

The Scottish artist Blackadder has composed her still-life using the paper as a flat surface, on which she has arranged many objects related to her theme of bamboo and gold. See how she has spread light and dark tones of colour and similar shapes over the paper to create links across the composition. What happens if you look at the painting upside-down?

Lighter and darker
What happens if you arrange all the dark objects at the top of the composition? Does it look top-heavy? Try turning the page around and see what you think.

PIERO DELLA FRANCESCA *The Nativity* c.1472

In this painting, the Italian Renaissance artist Piero shows the story of the birth of Jesus. Everyone is celebrating, even the ox and the ass, and a shepherd points to the Star of Bethlehem overhead. Look at how the heavenly characters – the angels and Jesus – are grouped on the left side of the painting, while the earthly characters – Mary, Joseph, the shepherds, and the animals – are grouped together on the right side. Notice how Mary's cloak links the two sides of the painting.

Telling the story

Paint a scene from your favourite book, film, fairy-tale, poem, or play, and, like Piero, use composition to tell the story.

Hidden lines

Piero della Francesca's angels are composed in a row across the painting. Imagine horizontal lines running through their heads, hands, and feet, and vertical lines through their figures and the folds of their clothes. The horizontal and vertical lines give the painting a feeling of stillness and calm.

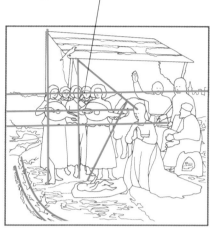

Leading our eyes

Can you imagine diagonal lines which lead your eyes to the most important people in the Nativity story? See how this group is encircled by a curving line?

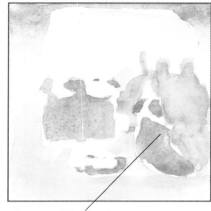

Story-telling colours

The people from Heaven are painted in sky blues and those from Earth in earth-colours. Mary's clothes are sky blue and earth red.

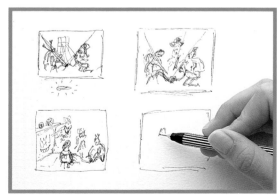

1 Sketch the characters in your story, experimenting with the way each one looks. Then try sketching them in different poses. Choose your favourites.

2 Make some small sketches to help you choose which composition and format works best. Decide what things to put into your painting and what to leave out.

3 Choose colours that will help you to express the meaning of your story best. Can you see what your story is about from the composition of your painting?

Painting nature

Whether you live in the city near a park, in the open countryside, or by the sea, there are always plenty of natural subjects to explore and paint. You might choose a broad view of nature where you look into the distance, a "landscape" or a "seascape", or a small, corner of nature such as a close-up study of flowers, wildlife, rocks, or reflections in water. Paintings of nature can also be imaginary, and the changing weather and seasons can suggest different moods and feelings.

Painting outside
Here are some practical tips for when you go painting outside:

- Pack a sketchbook, some paints, a small bottle of water, and a jar.

- Choose your natural subject.

- Find somewhere comfortable to sit.

- Rest the sketchbook on your knees.

- Make sure you keep the same viewpoint.

- If time is short, mix blobs of the colours you see or take a photograph.

Blossom
Nature can be painted close up by simply studying some flowers like this blossom.

Painting landscapes

When you are choosing a landscape to paint, think about the composition of your painting, and about space, colours, shape, pattern, and the amount of movement you would like to include. The captions around the landscape photograph opposite will help you.

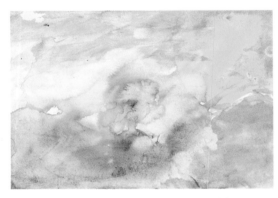

NATALIE (aged 9) *A Spring Day* 1993
Try painting the same landscape in each of the four seasons. The colours of the landscape change with the seasons and so do the shapes of trees and plants.

SAMIA (aged 9) *The Storm* 1993
If you want to paint a storm scene, you will have to use your imagination, as painting on the spot could be difficult! Listen to a piece of stormy music to inspire you.

Background
The background is the area furthest away from you. Notice how difficult it is to see details of things that are far-away.

Foreground
The foreground is the area closest to you. Things in the foreground seem larger and more detailed.

KAWAI GYOKUDO *Departing Spring* 1916

This Japanese landscape of a dramatic river gorge with a houseboat is part of a decorative screen. The artist, Kawai Gyokudo, tries to show how quickly spring passes by painting delicate blossom falling on to hard rocks. Notice the cool colours and the patches of gold leaf he has used to show the sunlight. The composition cuts out the sky and the distance, and focuses on nearby shapes and patterns in the rocks and the water.

JOSEPH MALLORD WILLIAM TURNER *Lake Nemi* c.1828

The British artist Turner painted this oil sketch on the spot, when he was travelling in Italy. He painted seven such compositions on one large canvas so that they could be carried back home more easily. Turner had to work quickly to capture the light on the lake before it changed, so he painted the scene with simple patches of colour without worrying about details.

Far-away colours
Have you noticed that things in the distance look paler – sometimes even blue? This is caused by moisture in the air. To create this effect of the light, painters in the past used a technique called "scumbling".

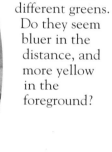

Try scumbling for yourself. Paint the distant scenery in shades of brown. Let it dry. Then paint a light wash of white over the top. It will look blue!

Shadows
Notice the patterns that the shadows make and think of the different ways you can paint them.

Figures
People and animals move, so sketch them quickly when you see them.

Weather
Colours and the light are affected by the weather and the time of day.

Horizon
The horizon is the line where the sky meets the ground.

Different greens
Look at all the different greens. Do they seem bluer in the distance, and more yellow in the foreground?

Middle ground
The middle ground is the area between the foreground and the background.

Using a viewfinder
Make a viewfinder with two L-shaped pieces of card. Use it to find and frame a part of the landscape that you feel will make an interesting composition. You can alter the format of your composition by adjusting the two pieces of card.

Feeding your imagination

Ideas for paintings can come from many sources, and sometimes even the strangest objects can inspire you to start a picture. It is worth making a collection of resources that catch your eye. These can feed your imagination and remind you of ideas and feelings. Sketches, poems, a diary, advertisements, and films are also good resources and you may find surprising links between unexpected things. All these things can suggest themes that you can develop in your paintings.

Creative doodlings
Have you ever seen images in random marks of paint or in blobs of ink? Try transforming these into a picture or an amusing character.

Painted stories
Create whole paintings from your random doodles.

Hidden ideas
Images found in patterned wallpaper, crumbling walls, stones, and clouds can help you invent landscapes with rivers, mountains, rocks, and trees, or portraits of expressive faces and quick-moving figures.

Anything is possible
Try creating surreal ("beyond the real") creatures by imagining seemingly impossible combinations of things like the one below.

Fantasy creatures
To make your creatures, combine odd photographs from magazines with things from your resources. Paint the weird results in a picture that tells a strange story.

SIDNEY NOLAN *Kelly and Sergeant Kennedy 1945*

The Australian, 20th-century artist Sidney Nolan painted a series of pictures about the bushranger (outlaw) Ned Kelly, who wore iron armour to protect himself from the police. Nolan used his imagination to create Kelly from a black square, and the policeman from a newspaper photograph, partly painted over. The composition is sharply divided by a tree; how does this help to tell the story in the painting?

LEONORA CARRINGTON *The House Opposite 1945*

The English Surrealist artist Carrington paints fantasy worlds where people, animals, and plants are magically transformed, as if in a dream. Here she arranges the space of her painting to show different things happening at the same time – potions are brewed and people change into trees, while sleepers dream in the attics.

Resources for pictures

Poems, fairy tales, myths, cultural legends, and news stories can feed you with ideas and subjects for paintings. As a child, Leonora Carrington enjoyed listening to mysterious Celtic stories, which inspired some of her paintings. Keep a diary of your ideas for paintings, and start a collection of resources like the one below to inspire you. The most fascinating collections are made gradually, over time.

Music
Sometimes a piece of music can help you to imagine your subject.

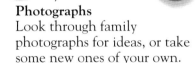

Photographs
Look through family photographs for ideas, or take some new ones of your own.

Works of art
Visit museums and galleries to research your ideas. Collect postcards of your favourite paintings.

Collecting colours
Different colour combinations and patterns often trigger ideas for paintings, too.

Collecting for a theme

When walking through your local area, collect anything that you feel reflects its character. Sift through this collection and then choose the best things for an imaginative collage "portrait" of the area where you live.

JACQUELINE PERCY *City Walk 1993*
This collage is made from strips of paper found on walks near the artist's home, with pastel and paint.

About the artists

Frank Auerbach (born 1931, British) was born in Germany, but has lived in England since he was seven. His favourite subjects are his local park and friends, which he paints using thick paint applied with brushes, knives, and his hands.

Gillian Ayres RA (born 1930, British) creates brightly coloured abstract paintings. She applies paint thickly, with strong movement of brushes and her fingers, overlaying colours and creating exciting textures.

Elizabeth Blackadder RA (born 1931, British) paints subjects around her home such as her collection of exotic toys and objects, flowers, and her pet cats. She makes careful arrangements of combinations of objects in her pictures.

Rosa Bonheur (1822-1899, French) was one of the most popular artists of her day. In her studio in a forest near Paris, she worked on large paintings of animals, especially lions, tigers, wolves, and horses.

Pierre Bonnard (1867-1947, French) painted ordinary subjects such as people at home, gardens, and street scenes. He loved colour and shape, and his paintings with their delicate brushwork are very atmospheric.

Leonora Carrington (born 1917, British) lives in Chicago and Mexico City. She is a Surrealist artist which means that she paints dreams and strange combinations of objects to create mysterious fantasy paintings. "Surreal" means "beyond the real".

Mary Cassatt (1845-1926, American) worked mainly in Paris and was a member of the Impressionist group. Like many of these artists, her paintings show that she admired the flat shapes and patterns of Japanese art.

Paul Cézanne (1839-1906, French) was first associated with the Impressionists. He mainly painted at his home in the South of France where, through studying nature, he discovered new ways of showing solid form.

Manohar Das (born c.1560, Indian) was one of the finest court painters to the Emperors of the Mughal dynasty in Northern India. He illustrated manuscripts with miniature portraits and colourful scenes from court life.

André Derain (1880-1954, French) was one of the main artists in the Fauve ("wild beast") group. His brightly coloured landscapes and seascapes were painted outdoors, near Paris and in the South of France.

George Grosz (1893-1959, German) began his career as a caricaturist. He lived in Berlin until after the First World War, then he moved to New York. He was especially critical of people's greed in his paintings.

Kawai Gyokudo (1873-1957, Japanese) painted poetic views of the landscape around Tokyo on to large decorative screens. His paintings recorded people going about their daily lives, and nature in different seasons and weather conditions.

Flavia Irwin (born 1916, British) lives in the country, and paints delicate abstract paintings inspired by the English and French countryside. She works from drawings and looks for the underlying structure of shapes in the landscape.

Edward Lear (1812-1888, British) was a famous children's writer and illustrator who wrote limericks and nonsense verse. He travelled to countries like Italy, Greece, and India, painting and sketching landscapes, people, animals, and birds as he went.

Leonardo da Vinci (1452-1519, Italian) was a genius of the Renaissance period, who was a great painter, sculptor, engineer, musician, and scientist. His fascinating sketchbooks show us his curiosity, inventiveness, and imagination at work.

Fra Filippo Lippi (c.1406-1469, Italian) was a Renaissance painter from Florence and a follower of Masaccio. They worked together on the wall painting shown on page 35. Lippi later developed his own delicate style of painting.

Tommaso Masaccio (1401-1428, Italian) lived near Florence during the Renaissance period. Although he died at the age of 27, his few paintings were a great influence on later artists like Piero della Francesca.

Claude Monet (1840-1926, French) was an Impressionist artist who tried to capture the way different light and weather conditions changed the appearance of nature. He painted many colourful images of his garden at Giverny.

Mutipuy (died 1970s, Australian) lived in West Arnhemland in northern Australia. He was one of the finest Aboriginal bark painters, using ochre colours to paint animals and figures, often in "X-ray" detail. Aboriginal artists use traditional ways of painting, going back over 30,000 years.

Sidney Nolan RA (1917-1993, Australian) painted many imaginative and sometimes funny images of Australian history. His paintings often show legendary people like the early explorers and bushrangers (outlaws), set in the bush or deserts of Australia.

Emil Nolde (1867-1956, German) was one of the German Expressionist artists. He used colour and distorted shapes to emphasize the feeling in his landscapes and religious pictures. He also painted vivid watercolours.

Jacqueline Percy (born 1943, British) lives and works in London and by the sea, making collages with found objects.

Pablo Picasso (1881-1973, Spanish) lived and worked in France where he became the most famous artist of the 20th century. He created new ways of portraying the world in his many paintings, sculptures, drawings, and ceramics.

Piero della Francesca (c.1410-1492, Italian) painted religious pictures for many churches near Florence. He was fascinated by composition and used geometry to construct his paintings.

Renaissance artists were painters and sculptors living in Europe between c.1450-1650 who were interested in the art of Ancient Greece and Rome. Renaissance means "rebirth". Masaccio, Piero della Francesca, Leonardo da Vinci and Michelangelo were all Renaissance artists.

Pierre Auguste Renoir (1841-1919, French) was one of the leading Impressionist painters. He mainly painted people, and tried to give an overall impression of a scene, rather than painting the fine detail.

Mark Rothko (1903-1970, American) was born in Russia, but lived and worked as an Abstract Expressionist painter in America. He used colours and shapes to express a mood or feeling instead of showing recognizable objects.

Albert Pinkham Ryder (1847-1917, American) lived most of his life in the city of New York, although his pictures were often of the sea or imaginary dream-like subjects. His paintings influenced many modern American artists.

Georges Seurat (1859-1891, French) invented Pointillism (painting with dots of separate colour). Although he died young, he painted many large compositions of people at leisure, landscapes, and seascapes.

Peggy Somerville (1918-1975, British) was famous for the confident drawings and paintings she created as a child. She painted and sketched from her imagination. Her favourite subjects were landscapes with gypsies, horses, or cows.

Georges de la Tour (1593-1652, French) was famous for the dramatic use of candlelight in his paintings. His everyday subjects and religious pictures are realistic, yet simple.

James Mallord William Turner (1775-1851, British) was a painter of landscapes and seascapes whose main interest was how to show the effects of light. His dramatic paintings show light during storms, fires, and sunsets.

Vincent van Gogh (1853-1890, Dutch) was born in The Netherlands, and moved to France where he did many of his most expressive paintings. In the eight years before his suicide, he created many landscapes, portraits, and still-lifes full of colour and movement.

Diego Rodriguez de Silva y Velazquez (1599-1660, Spanish) specialized in painting portraits, mostly of the Spanish Royal Family and other court characters. He is famous for creating wonderfully rich effects from very simple brushmarks and colours.

Edouard Vuillard (1868-1940, French) was a friend of Bonnard. He lived in Paris where he painted quiet, intimate scenes from everyday life which are full of subtle patterns and colours.

Emmanuel de Witte (1617-1692, Dutch) painted scenes from everyday life that are set in realistic interiors. He used light and shadow to create a sense of space, and his figures often enact a simple story.

Index

Acknowledgements

PICTURE CREDITS
Every effort has been made to trace the copyright holders of the paintings reproduced in this book and Dorling Kindersley apologizes in advance for any unintentional omissions. We would be pleased to insert the appropriate acknowledgement in any subsequent edition of this publication.

Key:
t: top b: bottom l: left r: right c: centre

Bibliotheque Nationale, Paris 10bl; The Bridgeman Art Library, London 8tc/Louvre, Paris/Giraudon 32bl; Jane Burton (cockerel) 25br; Dallas Museum of Art/ The Wendy and Emery Reves Collection 33tr; Mary Evans Picture Library 32tr; Glasgow Museums: Art Gallery & Museum, Kelvingrove/Woman in Blue with a Child, 1899, Edouard Vuillard, © DACS 1993, 27tr; Andy Crawford, 8bl, 36l(2nd boy); Rebecca Hossack Gallery 13br; The Houghton Library, Harvard University, Cover, 4bl; The Image Bank/Steve Dunwell 27bl; reproduced by kind permission of The Trustees of The Edward James Foundation, West Dean Estate, West Dean, Chichester, England /Serpentine Gallery Dec-Jan 1992, © 1993, Leonora Carrington/ARS, New York 43t; Colin Keates 10l, 26tl; Kunsthistorisches Museum, Vienna 19tr; © 1993 By The Metropolitan Museum of Art/Bequest Stephen C.Clark, 1960, 17b/ Gift of Cornelius Vanderbilt, 1887, 28bl/Bequest of Mrs H.O. Havemeyer, 1929, The H.O. Havemeyer Collection 35bl; reproduced by courtesy of the Trustees, The National Gallery, London 8c, 39tl; National Gallery of Art, Washington, © 1993 Kate Rothko–Prizel and Christopher Rothko/ARS, New York 20bl; National Museum of Modern Art, Tokyo 40bl; National Museum of American Art, Washington, D.C./Art Resource, NY, 18bl; Sir Sidney Nolan, OM RA, Kelly and Sergeant Kennedy, 1945, synthetic polymer paint on cardboard with paper collage 63.6 x 76.4cm, Collection: Nolan Gallery, Canberra, Australia, 42bl; Jacqueline Percy 43br; Sketchbook 172: Interior with Artist and Baboon Each Painting the Other, 1964, Pablo Picasso, © DACS 1993, 22bl; Susanna Price 10tr; Pierre Auguste Renoir, The Swing, © Photo R.M.N. 17tr; Tim Ridley 25br (shell and teapot) Royal Academy of Arts, London, 26br, 30b/Boats in the Port of Collioure, 1905, André Derain © ADAGP, Paris and DACS, London 1993, 15tl/The Hague 36bl /Collection of William A. Plapinger and Kathleen J. Murray 38bl/ Statens Museum, Copenhagen 21tr/John Theobold 8br; Royal Asiatic Society 25tr; The Royal Collection © 1993, Her Majesty Queen Elizabeth II 22br; Scala 35t; The Child Art of Peggy Somerville, published by Herbert Press, London 23tr; Southampton City Art Gallery, Two Dogs, 1891, Pierre Bonnard, © ADAGP/SPADEM, Paris and DACS, London 1993, 24bl; Carl Shone 27br; Steve Shott 36c (boys 1& 3); Tony Stone Images 37tl, 42tr/Michael Busselle 7cl, 40-41b; Tate Gallery, London 41tl; Thyssen-Bornemisza Collection/The Big City, 1916-17, George Grosz, © DACS 1993, 37tr; Collection of Mrs. John Hay Whitney 29tl; Peter Wood 13tr; Jerry Young 25br (peacock and elephant).

The authors would like to thank the following for their help: Sue Unstead, Linda Cole, Mary Anne Stevens, Ally Scott, Paula Kitt, Sara Gordon, Lisa Bass, Gina Slade, Peter Feroze, Helen Valentine, Emma Lindsey, Sue Carpenter, Tim Curle, Alec Chanda, Jill Bennett, Claire Biggart, Liz White, Penny Konig, Marilyn Barnes, Felix Hilton, John Theobold, and the children of Thomas' Preparatory School, The Unicorn School, Grinling Gibbons School, St. James's Independent School, Henry Fawcett Primary Schools.

Dorling Kindersley would like to thank Cornelissen's for the loan of the muller; Sharon Peters, Jane Horne, Sara Nunan, Monica Byles, Stella Love, Dawn Sirrett, Mandy Earey, and Jonathan Buckley for their help in the production of this book, and Marvin Campbell, Pui-Shan Chan, Stacie Terry, Andrew Abello, Joseph Duncombe, Andrea East, William Lion, Annette Afflick, Danny Cole, Darren Chin, and Katie King for appearing in its pages.

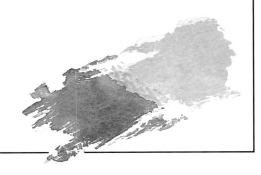

ELIZABETH WATERS is Education Officer for the Royal Academy of Arts in London, where she organizes educational programmes to coincide with the Royal Academy's major exhibitions – writing gallery guides and leading gallery tours for students and teachers, and working with artists-in-residence to run workshops for children, which combine the history and practice of art. Elizabeth studied History of Art at the University of Kent at Canterbury. She is married to a painter and lives in London.

ANNIE HARRIS is a painter and lecturer and exhibits her work in a London gallery. As an artist-in-residence at the Royal Academy of Arts, she has led many practical workshops and gallery tours for primary and secondary school children. Born in Australia, Annie studied Italian Literature at Sydney University and worked in children's publishing before graduating in Fine Art from Camberwell School of Arts and Crafts in London. She is married with two children and lives in London.

THE ROYAL ACADEMY OF ARTS (Painting, Sculpture, Architecture, and Engraving), was founded in 1768 and is the oldest Fine Arts Institution in Great Britain. It is best known today for its major exhibitions and its annual Summer Exhibition of contemporary art. Its educational mission is demonstrated by The Royal Academy Schools, which run post-graduate course for students, and the Education Department, which organizes In-House and Outreach programmes for the general public and schools.